MW00912310

ALIENS

WRITTEN BY CHRISTOPHER KENWORTHY

ILLUSTRATED BY ROGER O'REILLY

M·Q·P

CONTENTS

SIGHTINGS

SKYWATCHER

A large UFO was seen by ten witnesses off Highway 53 in Minnesota. Metallic in appearance, it was spotted by Dave Briscoe, the local director of UFO group Skywatch. He watched the craft for three minutes, while others saw it for almost 15. There were no lights visible on it, but the edge of the ship was marked with dark points. It appeared from nowhere, and hovered silently. It's just possible that it was taking an interest in the recent showing of *Independence Day*, because it hovered near to a local cinema. When it left, it headed towards the port of Duluth, before shooting vertically into the sky.

MISIDENTIFICATION

During the hours of darkness, it's easy to mistake satellites, meteors, aircraft and planets for UFOs. At night, witnesses have a greater tendency to panic, overeact and imagine details which aren't actually present. Many serious researchers estimate that 95 per cent of all reported UFO sightings are nothing other than misidentifications. In late 1995, a UFO researcher

from Lancashire found out how true these statistics are, when a woman reported a UFO hovering over nearby fields. She said that she'd seen it when she went into a restaurant, and that it was still there when she left two hours later. Circular, with bright green lights and an unearthly glow, she believed that it was sinister, and felt it was watching her. A very short investigation revealed that it was nothing other than a local motorway service station, decked out with new lighting!

DAYLIGHT

UFOs seen in daylight are more impressive than those viewed at night, as misidentification is much less likely. One of the best recent cases occurred in February 1997, when residents of Takapuna, New Zealand witnessed a huge UFO. The silvery-grey object with a rotating rim was seen in a clear sky, in broad daylight by many people. Accounts such as these are important, they are more detailed than reports of blurred lights in the sky. We've all seen hundreds of UFO clips of fuzzy blobs filmed at night – these are easily dismissed by sceptics. UFO researchers are waiting for video footage of a solid alien craft, viewed in daylight and, if the New Zealand incident is anything to go by, we may not have long to wait.

MULTIPLE WITNESSES

Some of the best UFO cases involve multiple witnesses. The possibility of having one over-excited witness can be ruled out when several people report seeing the same object. One case occurred on September 15th 1996, in Surrey, British Columbia, when nine people saw a UFO event lasting half an hour. A flashing object, said to look like a star, was seen moving erratically in the sky, continually returning to a stationary point between two other lights. The same night, a huge object, twice the size

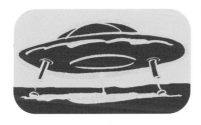

of a 747, was reported in the area. More recently, on March 4th 1997, a 100 metre (approximately 300 feet) wide silver saucer was seen by hundreds of people in Piracicaba, Brazil.

JELLY UFOs

The alien 'craft' seen by witnesses don't always resemble nuts and bolts spaceships. Sometimes they are more like jelly or gas, and change shape as they move. A man from British Columbia was witness to such a UFO in early 1997, floating above Burnaby Mountain. It appeared to be a bright light at first, about 60 metres (200 feet) above the tree line. At one point a beam of light flashed from its side, and then it elongated, before resuming its original shape. Some researchers believe this stretching might be connected with a UFO's propulsion system which allows it to warp space.

STAR TREKKING

William Shatner, who played Captain Kirk in *Star Trek*, once witnessed a UFO. He claims that it helped to rescue him from a deadly situation. While motor-cycling across a desert with friends in the sixties, Shatner became separated from the group and ran out of fuel. Afraid and alone he began to fear that he might die of thirst, but then he saw a UFO. He described it as a silver-glowing disc hovering above the horizon. He doesn't remember what happened next, but before long he was back with his friends, safe again. Whatever the UFO was, he is certain that it helped to transport him away from danger.

BEATLEMANIA

John Lennon of The Beatles told several stories of paranormal activity, and hinted at more than one UFO sighting. The most famous, however, is the time when he saw a classic cigar-shaped UFO hovering over a river. It was this sighting that led him to write, 'There's UFOs over New York and I ain't too surprised', in his song *Strange Days Indeed*.

ELECTION PROMISES

Some Ufologists suspect that all American presidents know about UFOs, and have seen recovered craft and footage of alien contact. Former president Jimmy Carter is one of the only ones to admit having seen a UFO. He reported the incident long before he became president. The sighting occurred in Leary, Georgia, after dark on January 6th 1969. Carter was standing outdoors, when he saw a self-luminous object, brighter than the moon. He reported that there were ten other witnesses, and that the object moved towards and away from him several times. The experience prompted him to state publicly during his election campaign, that if he became president he would make UFO information available to the public. Sadly, like so many pre-election promises this one wasn't kept. Conspiracy theorists suggest that this is because he is covering up a government deal with aliens.

ROYAL UFOs

Lord Mountbatten, the Queen's cousin, is said to have witnessed a UFO. He was known to be a fan of the subject, and there are many stories relating to a UFO which is alleged to have landed on his Broadlands estate. Some serious researchers of Ufology firmly believe this is true, and state that a craft landed and that its occupants conversed with a member of Mountbatten's staff. A former Lord Mayor of London has also alleged that Mountbatten told him that the British government had recovered an alien craft, and were storing it in a secret base in Wales.

ALIEN SQUADRON

A World War II sighting left sergeant Stephen J. Brickner of the 1st Marine Division stunned. He was camped in a tropical area, on the lookout for Japanese fighters, when an air-raid warning was sounded. Hiding in his foxhole, Brickner lay on his back, watching the sky. A formation of 150 wingless objects passed overhead, with a mighty roar. He said that the sound was louder and more rumbling than that of Japanese planes, and that instead of flying in 'v' formation, they flew in lines of ten objects, faster than Japanese planes. The sergeant also noticed that the UFOs seemed to be undergoing spatial distortion, because they appeared to wobble, as though dematerialising; the effect made their highly-polished silver hulls shimmer in the sun.

WATCHED BY ALIENS

A resident of Salt Lake City, Utah, was returning home on January 19th 1997, when he saw a pulsing orange light in the sky above a neighbour's house. He signalled frantically to his wife, and the UFO seemed to respond to his gesture. As he pointed at it, the light shot to the east at great speed. It hovered in that position for a while, then moved gradually away and then blinked out. The couple waited for a while longer, and saw an identical object flying in the same area of sky. When the man moved his arm to point at it, the object froze in place. The couple felt like they were being watched, and were alarmed to see the first light reappear where it had vanished minutes before. A 747 jet was also flying in the same air space and the couple saw the UFO fly within about 100 metres (approximately 300 feet) of it. Following this near miss, the UFO travelled slowly, pulsing, until it was just about one and a half kilometres (approximately one mile) from the couple's house. At this point the object sparkled and elongated; sparks shot out of it for a few seconds and then it disappeared from view.

CHILE WAVE

A wave of UFO sightings occurred in Chile, during February 1997. Motorists stopped on roads to the north of Santiago de Chile to look at an elongated cloud. After a few minutes it split into two objects, which came together to form a giant cigar-shaped UFO. This object split into four smaller cigar-shapes. Witnesses say that this splitting and reforming went on for some time,

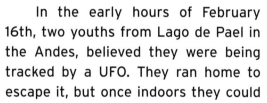

before four objects flew away together at high speed.

In the early hours of February 16th, two youths from Lago de Pael in the Andes, believed they were being tracked by a UFO. They ran home to escape it, but once indoors they could still see it. They dragged their father our of bed, and he joined them at the window, where they saw the landed craft. An alien just over one metre (approximately four feet) tall, was standing outside the ship. It had a large hairless head and was wearing a blue suit. The family were so frightened that they hid until it went away. On February 24th a ring shaped craft was seen hovering over a lake. The next day a UFO was reported to have entered restricted airspace, where the Chilean Air Force's aerobatics team was performing. This UFO was described as being like a bright smoke-ring, which drifted away at the speed of a car. It was filmed by at least two people.

TRIANGULAR CRAFT

Triangular-shaped UFOs are now seen as often as saucers and spheres. They started to become common after multiple-witness sightings of a huge black triangle over Belgium in 1989. It has been seen on many occasions since − often by police, and shows up on radar. The earliest report of a triangle UFO is from 1950, in the town of La Crescenta, California. On the morning of March 10th, many people saw the triangle fly over the town at about 1500 metres (approximately 5000 feet).

FIERY PHOENIX

In Phoenix, Arizona, Norm Miller and his family saw about eight round lights, on the evening of May 9th 1997. The lights clustered together, then moved into and out of 'v' formations, before regathering as a cluster. Less than a week later, residents of nearby Sunnyslope and Squaw Peak saw a large boomerang-shaped UFO which was covered in white lights. Then on June 23rd orange balls of light were videotaped by multiple witnesses across Arizona. In one case the balls of light were seen to be lined up in a row. Although radar couldn't pick up the objects, thousands of people were reported to have observed them.

SUBMARINE UFO

Two friends on the South American Island of Guyana watched a UFO dive into the ocean on the evening of June 12th 1997. It was a cloudless night when they saw the object which flew at great speed, before diving into the sea. It slipped into the water without making a sound. UFOs have sometimes been seen rising from beneath the water, and there have also been reports of bright lights seen skimming below the surface of the ocean at amazing speed.

TOTAL ECLIPSE

During a total eclipse of the sun, in Minnesota, two friends were witness to several UFOs. Eight circular objects, with red lights on their perimeters, appeared in  the distance, and flew over the witnesses. The path the UFOs followed was from the moon, towards the Hale-Bopp comet – also in the sky at the time. The second witness claimed to have seen the same object seven years earlier. On the same day, a witness in British Columbia was watching the Hale-Bopp comet, and saw three white lights flying about six times faster than a jet. Just prior to the sighting, his video camera had gone dead, so he was unable to secure footage. UFOs are often sighted during solar eclipses, or within a few days of them. Some ancient prophecies suggest that the aliens will make themselves known to us during an eclipse at sacred sites in southern England, during July 1999.

ENEMY INVASION

During World War II, unidentified disc-shaped craft were seen flying over Los Angeles, and were fired on by American troops. The incident occurred on February 25th 1942, and 1430 rounds of anti-aircraft ammunition were fired at the objects. No bombs were dropped from the hovering lights, which seems to rule out an enemy attack. One of the discs floated quite low, while shells impacted off its hull without causing damage. The craft moved along the coast at about nine-and-a-half kilometres (approximately six miles) an hour, before vanishing. During the aerial display, small, highly mobile red lights were also seen dodging the ammunition. Six people were killed from debris and shell damage, and three others died of heart attacks during the panic. Although there were multiple witnesses to the UFOs, the Navy declared the incident a false alarm.

HOUSTON, WE HAVE A PROBLEM

There are many rumours surrounding the Apollo 11 mission to the moon, concerning UFOs. Although none are substantiated by firm evidence, many Ufologists believe that Neil Armstrong and Buzz Aldrin were witness to alien craft. It is rumoured that soon after landing on the moon, 'other spacecraft' were seen in the vicinity of the Eagle landing module. The craft were said to have landed on the rim of a nearby crater. A day later, an object was apparently seen between the orbiting module and the moon. The description sounds similar to a glowing disc which was seen by the crew of Apollo 8, when they orbited the moon on Christmas day 1968. It is because of this first sighting, that UFOs are supposedly referred to as 'Santa Claus' by NASA. Four months after the first landing, Apollo 12 made it to the moon, and was said to have seen two flashing objects, one on either side of the spaceship. Observatories in Europe who were watching the space-craft, also saw these lights. As in many of these cases, mysterious radio noise was heard. When travelling back to earth, the crew were reported to have seen a bright red object. Unexplained flashes of light were also seen by the crews of Apollo 16 and 17 and Gemini 7.

SPACEMAN

On May 15th 1963, Major Gordon Cooper blasted into space in the Mercury capsule. Before returning to earth, he contacted the Australian tracking station at Mechea near Perth, to tell them that he had seen a green, glowing object ahead of him. The station picked up the UFO with its radar, and tracked it approaching the Mercury capsule at great speed. When Cooper landed, reporters were told that questions regarding the UFO would not be permitted.

COSMIC THING

Cosmonauts flying on the Voshkod I mission in 1964, were overtaken by flying discs. The Soviets apparently admitted to seeing an 'unmanned satellite' just under one kilometre (approximately half a mile) from Voshkod II a year later. There are rumours that the 'satellite' was in fact a UFO, which harassed the cosmonauts. Soon after the sighting the capsule lost contact with ground control and began an emergency landing, reaching earth a considerable distance from the planned recovery site.

UFO WINDOWS

Areas where UFOs visit time after time are known as 'windows'. There are many UFO windows around the world, sometimes they are just are relatively small, but at other times they can be almost the size of a continent. UFO windows sometimes close, and there are no sightings for years. When one opens there may be hundreds of sightings in a couple of weeks, before it closes again. Some windows open only once, but others have been active over many years, such as the one over Bonnybridge, in Scotland, and Wiltshire in England. The only part of the world with almost no reported windows is Africa. UFO windows sometimes appear over cities, but can also occur in remote areas such as the Nullarbor Plain in Australia. Stone circles and ancient sites, such as Stonehenge, are thought to be mini-windows, that attract huge numbers of UFOs every year.

LEY LINES

Using pendulums and metal rods, dowsers have found an energy grid of power-lines all over earth. These 'ley

lines' are said to attract UFOs, and run between monuments, churches and tumuli, often for vast distances. One of the most famous lines runs right across southern England. It starts at Lands End, passing through 50 sacred sites, runs on to the East Anglian coast covering sites such as Glastonbury Tor and the Avebury Stone Circle. Ancient sites such as pyramids, stone circles, medicine wheels, shrines, cathedrals, holy wells, burial mounds, chalk horses and churches, are often found in these alignments. UFOs tend to appear in the vicinity of ley lines, especially where they cross, at sights such as Stonehenge in Wiltshire. This area was one of the first to be patterned with crop circles in the early eighties; some people believe that the occupants of UFOs use crop circles to recharge ley lines and harmonise our planet.

FOO FIGHTERS

Although many UFOs were seen during World War II, the term 'flying saucer' hadn't yet been coined, and the glowing lights were known as 'foo fighters'. The word 'foo' derives from '*feu*' the French word for fire, the name was adopted as many of the sightings occurred over France. In 1942, William J. Methorst was onboard a ship near New Guinea, watching for enemy aircraft at noon. Through his binoculars he saw a large glowing disc, at about 1500 metres (approximately 5000 feet), moving rapidly. The UFO circled the ship for over three hours, and was tracked constantly. It disappeared at tremendous speed, estimated at about 4800 kilometres (approximately 3000 miles) an hour. The pilot of a Hurricane interceptor, B.C. Lumsden, saw 'foos' over France in December 1942. They looked like balls of orange light, and flew with one above the other, moving slowly and growing brighter as he watched. When attempting to get a better view, the objects followed him, always remaining behind his aeroplane. Lumsden dived about 900 metres (approximately 3000 feet) and the lights followed him again for a while, before leaving him alone. His story was mocked, until another pilot had a similar experience days later. In 1944 a B-29 returning from a mission in Sumatra was paced by a spherical object, no more than two metres (approximately six feet) wide. It throbbed with red light, and followed the plane's every move for eight minutes, before giving up the chase and accelerating away. Other foos were described as crystal balls, the size of footballs, which would fly up to a squadron and then follow it. Unlike other UFOs they always appeared to be small, without occupants, and there are no reports of the foos landing.

SHEFFIELD TRIANGLE

If aliens really are visiting earth, they don't appear to be very good pilots considering the number of crashes they have. Although the Roswell incident is the most famous crash of an alien saucer, there have been numerous other reports from around the world. Several have taken place in Britain, with one spectacular incident in March 1997. A loud booming noise was heard in South Yorkshire, as confirmed by detectors at Edinburgh University. Two men claim to have seen a black triangular-shaped UFO fly over their house just before the noise occurred. The craft had a light at each tip, and a blue light in the centre, and the witnesses claim that it was followed by several RAF jets, sparking rumours that the UFO may have been shot down. Others suggest that the triangle was simply a secret stealth-type aeroplane being tested at night, and that the noise was a sonic boom. There is evidence, however, to suggest that something did crash — when a UFO investigator headed towards the area where the UFO seemed to have come down a police roadblock prevented them from making any further investigation.

BEDROOM **VISITS**

Chilean mother of two, Marta Aguilar reported being woken one night in February 1997 by a crackling noise.

 Thinking that the sound might be static from the television set she turned to look at it, but instead saw an alien just over one metre (approximately four feet) tall. It was wearing a tight suit, a helmet and a backpack. She remained motionless, and the alien made no move towards her or the two children who were sharing the room. After several minutes, the static noise returned, and the alien walked through a wall. It's silhouette remained for a second, then vanished.

LEATHER CLAD ALIENS

Daoud Ahmad was woken by strange aliens while sleeping in his Nur-a-Shamat camp on the West Bank. The incident occurred in late December 1996. He awoke conscious of a threatening presence, as he tried to get out of bed, two creatures attacked him. Just over half a metre (approximately two feet) tall each alien had only one eye. Dressed in black leather, they were extremely strong, and beat Ahmad unconscious. The incident could be dismissed as a dream, except he was treated in hospital for severe facial bruising and neighbours reported hearing the attack take place.

TALL ALIENS

Shepherds in Spain have been reporting encounters with tall alien beings, since late February 1997.

Heliodoro Nunez was watching his flock at Paradeseca in the late afternoon, when his dogs were worried by something behind him. He turned to see three 'strange beings' about three metres (approximately ten feet) tall, wearing conical hats; they changed colour from red, through blue, yellow and green as he watched. At about the same time a neighbour, Juan Gonzalez Gonzalez saw an intense red light hovering over the treetops.

SNOW GATHERING

A Tibetan mountain climber stumbled across a UFO and its occupants on June 15th 1974. Keo Wha Unan was studying rocks in a cave high up on the Himalayan Mount Dahjar. Coming out of the cave he saw a silver disc hovering behind nearby rocks. There were no windows, ridges or markings on the craft, which hovered about one metre (approximately four feet) above ground. Three thin humanoids with light-grey skin were standing by the craft, and appeared to be gathering rocks, snow and ice. A device was lowered to retrieve the aliens, the craft began to hum and it rose a little before disappearing into the clouds.

CLOSE ENCOUNTER

Following a week of UFO sightings in Indiana, during May 1997, a flying saucer was seen at close quarters in Bloomington. Three people in a car saw eight UFOs blink into existence in front of them. The driver flashed his headlights to attract the UFOs, and two of them approached his position, moving in silently. The car's power went dead as one of the objects hovered overhead. One of the witnesses saw that the surface of the disc-shaped object was metallic, with a dome on top. The blue glow coming from the saucer was bright enough to light up the road beneath it, and the air under the saucer sparkled and shimmered. The craft tilted slightly, and one witness saw through the side windows, and spotted creatures with large heads. Two spheres came out of the ship, and at that point the UFO levelled off and flew away. UFOs approach cars more than any other man-made objects, and in almost all cases the car engine cuts out.

APPROACHING ROSWELL

The flying-disc crash at Roswell, New Mexico in 1947 didn't come out the blue — there had been sightings of UFOs over the USA in the months leading up to the incident. In early May a silver object disintegrated over Washington State, and two weeks later, a flat, cigar-shaped object was seen at sunset by multiple witnesses in Richmond, Virginia. On the next day, May 19th, people in Manitou Springs, Colorado saw a silver object approach, hover, and then perform impossible aerobatics before flying away. On June 10th at Douglas, Arizona, a woman saw a spherical light rise over the Mexican border.

The Roswell crash itself is the most famous UFO incident. According to many witnesses, a 'flying disc' crashed north of Roswell on July 2nd 1947, leaving debris scattered over a huge area. There is no doubt that *something* crashed in the desert, and that the military recovered the material. Astonishingly, the US Air Force admitted they had recovered a flying disc. They retracted this story the next day, and claimed the debris was wreckage from a weather balloon. This seems unlikely, however, as witnesses described the debris as a lightweight metal, covered in hieroglyphics, which recovered its shape when bent. Researchers believe that small, grey alien bodies were recovered from the disc itself, and that the US government is trying to keep this story under wraps. Circumstantial evidence backs up these claims: a local funeral director was asked to provide small coffins just after the crash. Some people believe that several aliens survived, and were kept at Area 51 for several years.

UFOs ARE REAL

Documents released under the Freedom of Information Act, prove that Iranian pilots encountered UFOs in September 1976. The Imperial Iranian Air Force Command Post was contacted by worried citizens, who saw a bright light flying over Tehran. An F-4 fighter plane was sent to intercept the UFO and closed in upon a bright object ahead. At a distance of about 40 kilometres (approximately 25 miles) the pilot lost all instrumentation, and his radios went dead. He turned his plane around, and his equipment began to function normally. A second F-4 was sent to intercept, and picked up the UFO on radar. The craft was closing quickly, and was estimated to be as large as a tanker. A glowing object was seen leaving the first UFO, heading for the F-4 at great speed. The pilot attempted to fire a missile but his control panel went dead. He dived to escape, and the two UFOs rejoined. At this point a third UFO left the main craft and descended rapidly, and landed, casting light over a huge area. The pilot returned to the airport, and on final approach saw a cylindrical UFO with lights at either end, but the tower could not locate it with radar. No trace of the landing site was ever found, but locals reported seeing bright lights. The official report into this sighting was sent to the CIA, the National Security Agency and various defence bodies. It is regarded as one of the best contact cases, because there were multiple sightings, military interaction, radar traces, a landing, and official confirmation. Given all of the evidence it seems impossible to deny that UFOs are real.

UFO ABDUCTION

Stories of abduction vary slightly, but there are many consistencies. People report being taken from bedrooms, cars, remote places, and even cities. Although methods can vary greatly, the victim is usually completely paralysed, and the aliens are very often small, light-skinned beings, with huge, bald heads and large, black, almond-shaped eyes. They are known as Greys. The abductee is taken aboard the alien craft, and undergoes various tests. In most cases probes are used to remove semen from men, and eggs from women. Genetic material is harvested from abductees with alarming regularity. Following abduction, the victim may be returned to a location some distance from where they were taken away. In other cases they are returned to their original location, and only suffer from a slight feeling of disorientation.

MASK MEMORIES

Most abductees have no immediate memory of their experience. Somehow the memory has been hidden away, and it takes time for it to resurface. In cases of bedroom abduction, where the victim is floated or dragged from their sleeping place, the kidnapping can go undetected for years. At most, the abductee may feel unusual or tense the following morning. In roadside abductions, the memory isn't usually masked as effectively, perhaps because the victim was initially awake. Sometimes the abductee remembers seeing strange lights, even full-blown UFOs, before finding a period of missing time. Only when certain clues, such as scars, nightmares and nosebleeds prompt the victim into receiving hypnotism is the full memory uncovered. Somehow, until that point, the memory has been completely stifled. Although thousands of people claim to be abducted by aliens every year, their stories are often dreamlike. One reason for this may be that mask memories have been deliberately implanted into the victims' brains, to prevent them recalling the true experience. Such screen memories have been hinted at for years, but they are now becoming an important factor of UFO contact cases, and could explain many mysteries and discrepancies. People remember aliens dancing, playing games, performing mundane tasks or making bizarre statements. In one case a witness even claimed to have seen aliens performing the conga in her apartment!

MISSING TIME

Periods of time that cannot be accounted for, known as 'missing time', may indicate that an alien abduction has taken place. Missing time often occurs when people have been out alone, especially when driving in the country. Sometimes half an hour may be missing, although people have been known to lose up to eight hours. The discovery of missing time indicates that the memory has been wiped. Hypnosis can be used to help people to recover their memories of being abducted.

IMPLANTS

Many abductees report finding metallic implants inside their bodies, which they believe were put there by aliens. Implants are usually located in the nasal cavity, which explains why abductees often experience nosebleeds. In recent years, implants have also been found in other parts of the body, including the back of the neck, hands and feet. Some abductees have found that when their skin is exposed to ultra violet light, certain areas glow, and these 'indicator patches' show where an implant has been embedded. Implants may be used to monitor an individual's location, to make further abductions easier, or perhaps as bugging devices to monitor conversations and actions. It is even possible that implants may help to suppress memories of the actual abduction experience. In most cases up until 1995, implants were believed to dissolve as soon as an individual became aware of them.

MILITARY MEMORIES

Several years ago, a curious abduction case arose in Wiltshire, England. Three people experienced missing time which was associated with black military helicopters. The abductees believed they were taken away by the military, rather than aliens. All three experienced nosebleeds, headaches, and sensations of implants, but they believed they were the victims of a military exercise. Some conspiracy theorists agree, and say that for some unknown reason the military is abducting people. This could be part of a genetic experiment, or part of a secret deal with aliens. If this is true, then it could be the military which is implanting abductees with memories of bizarre aliens, so that when they tell their story it will seem laughably ridiculous.

NO DOOR

It is rare for abductees to remember being taken into the spacecraft, even when recalling the experience under hypnosis. Most people can recall details of the spacecraft's exterior, but their next memory is of being inside the craft. Some researchers say that if an abductee tells a detailed story, which includes a memory of entering the UFO, you can be certain that they've made the story up. In genuine abductions, nobody remembers going through the door.

FLUID TANKS

In the past few years abductees have reported seeing the results of genetic experiments. They are shown alien babies, or human babies in tanks, and sometimes strange hybrid children. Irene Rea described being abducted at about age three. She saw a grey man at the foot of her bed on many occasions, and associated his appearance with feeling drugged, and often felt ill the morning after. She also noticed a strange sound, and felt paralysed in his presence. She remembers being taken by several grey men into a room lined with tanks, each containing fluid and small babies. This description is quite common amongst abductees; the babies don't seem to be born in the normal way, but are grown in tanks.

HEALING ALIENS

Vancouver woman Alvena Scoott awoke in the night to see a tall, blue-eyed creature in her bedroom. The next thing she knew she was surrounded by more of the creatures in a white room. When she woke the next morning there was blood on her sheets and torso. A kidney complaint that she had suffered from prior to the abduction subsequently cleared up. Five years later she was abducted again, this time by insect-like aliens. She was taken against her will, in a state of paralysis. On board the craft she saw 20 other humans of both sexes. The aliens told her, via telepathy, that the women were to have sperm injected into them. Three months after the abduction she experienced a miscarriage, even though she was celibate.

ALIEN ZOOS

Aliens are rumoured to be creating 'survival zoos'. There is evidence to suggest that UFOs have appeared throughout the centuries, and are storing genetic material to prevent extinction of various species, including humans. The zoos may contain all of earth's important life forms, including those that are currently extinct, such as dinosaurs. Betty Andreasson of Massachusetts claims to have been abducted and placed inside a fluid-filled disc, which she believes took her to an underground cavern. Inside this natural setting, she saw strange cube-like crystals, each containing an unconscious human. She observed people from many eras and races, suggesting that this was a harvest of all types of human. She also saw cats, dogs, trees and birds, all frozen in time.

NAVEL GAZING

A woman from Indiana, experienced a classic abduction, even though she had no prior knowledge of UFOlogy. This rules out the suggestion that she may have been influenced by movies or TV images. While pregnant, she was abducted near a town called Abington, and recalls being clamped on a table with her legs apart. The Grey aliens told her that she wouldn't be hurt, but they inserted a humming instrument into her, which filled her with cramping pains. She was in a state of shock following the abduction, believing that her pregnancy had been affected. A subsequent visit to her doctor showed that the baby was gone, leaving no trace, as though she had been emptied out.

In further regression hypnosis she recalled that the Greys had shown her jars of fluid, with alien babies in them. She said they looked liked typical five or six-month-old foetuses, except that their heads were slightly enlarged. She said they had human-looking hands and feet, and even a navel. The presence of a navel is significant, because most reports of Greys say they have none, which suggests they are cloned rather than born. If these alien-human babies seen in the fluid jars really exist, it seems that aliens are using human mothers for the first stage of development.

ALIEN BABY

During a seven-hour TV special on UFOs, Mexican viewers were shown a baby which was said to be the product of human and alien hybridisation. The story goes that a Mexican girl was abducted by aliens, examined with a metal probe, and soon after found herself pregnant. She gave birth prematurely to a baby with black, almond-shaped eyes, just like a Grey alien's. Apparently, its skin was covered in scaly, reptilian-like flesh. The alien baby is now being looked after by local nuns.

WHAT DO THEY WANT?

Some people believe that aliens are the next stage of human evolution, and have travelled back in time to collect data on their former evolutionary state. Others think that abductions occur because aliens want to feel our emotions. In most abduction cases, the aliens appear to be emotionless, and some believe they may be adapting their offspring with our DNA, so that they can have our capacity for love and joy.

MEN IN BLACK

Men In Black (MIBs) are mysterious people who visit witnesses following UFO encounters. Some believe that they are CIA or National Security Agents, sent to threaten and silence contactees. Others note that there is a strangely alien atmosphere surrounding the Men In Black – they often speak in broken English with strange accents, and have pale grey skin.

A recent theory suggests Men In Black are never physically present, but are an implanted memory. It is possible that abductees are implanted with a belief in the Men In Black scenario, which lies dormant until they tell the story of their UFO encounter. Although a challenging idea, this could explain why abductees are the only ones to see MIBs; their neighbours and friends rarely see the mysterious figures. Men In Black most frequently appear in groups of three, but they have been known to appear alone, or in groups of two and four. They often carry briefcases, and frequently claim to be Air Force UFO Investigators, even though the Air Force say that no such research is carried out. During meetings with MIBs, people often feel disorientated, and are left feeling tired or dizzy.

SHUTTLE CRAFT

The space shuttle Discovery filmed an object, which many people believe was a UFO, on September 15th 1991. The footage shows a large, glowing object appearing over the earth's horizon (some estimates show that it was moving at great speed over Western Australia). There is a bright flash of light on the surface of earth, the UFO pauses and then shoots off into space at incredible speed. Moments later bolts of energy shoot up from two separate locations in Australia. These streaks of light pass through the space where the object was flying, as though trying to shoot it down.

Although some sceptics have claimed that the objects are merely particles of ice moving about in space, such a simple explanation does not explain the intelligent movement of the UFO. There is little doubt that the craft changes direction in response to the flash beneath it. To some people, this is video evidence of the highest calibre, because it was taken from a government owned space ship, rather than by an amateur photographer.

The chilling question is, why are covert bases on earth shooting at UFOs? Is there a secret war between our governments and aliens? Are we fending off abductors, or alien spies? We are told that Star Wars military technology never came to fruition, but this video suggests that it may well have done...

MASS MUTILATORS

Since 1967 there have been over 10000 well-documented cases of cattle mutilation linked to UFOs. In each case, there is no obvious cause of death, organs are removed with surgical precision, apparently using a high-temperature cutting device. There is never evidence of a struggle, and no blood is found on the grass. Sometimes the animal's body has been completely drained of blood, without a drop being spilt. No human has ever been found to be involved with cattle mutilation. The mutilations occur in areas of high UFO activity, and strange lights are often seen in the area days prior to the incident.

HORSE PLAY

One of the earliest cases of animal mutilation was also one of the most dramatic. In September 1967, a mutilated colt was found in Alamosa, Colorado. The animal's head had been completely stripped of flesh, and its brain, spine, lungs, heart and thyroid gland were all missing. Radioactivity in the area was slightly raised. A pathologist who examined the animal said that the

wounds appeared to be cauterised — in 1967 equipment capable of such a task was rare. There were no tracks near the carcass, but a set of 15 circular marks were found about twelve metres (approximately 40 feet) away. This is one of the few cases where physical evidence indicates that a UFO may have landed close to an animal, prior to attacking it.

MUTILATIONS

In the late seventies, a dairy farm near the town of Casino, Australia suffered a two-year period of cattle mutilations. Farm manager Barry Patch remembers finding a number of his cows mysteriously slaughtered. Most of them were found on one particular hillside. 'Udders would be removed, and various mutations formed there,' he said, 'but the carcass itself was quite complete. And there was no blood.' Of the 30 cows that were killed, most were about to calve, which suggests that the killers may have been taking an interest in reproduction and genetics. The deaths were apparently instantaneous, and Patch said, 'Some of the animals had mouthfuls of grass, when they came to an absolute sudden stop.' A vet who saw all the carcasses stated that causes of death were never determined. There were no bullet wounds, stab marks, needle punctures, poisons, or snake bites. Where tissue was removed from the bone, it was done far more cleanly than could be achieved with a knife. Barry Patch has no idea what caused the mutilations, but does claim to have seen UFOs over his farm.

UFO RESIDUE

A flaky white material was found on a cow's rib-cage following a case of UFO related mutilation in January 1993. The substance was also found on the ground near to the carcass, even though there were no traces of blood. Investigators took samples of the substance from the scene which they stored in a packet. When some of the flakes were removed they came into contact with the brass tip of a pen, and immediately melted into a clear liquid. The remaining flakes were tested and were found to contain deposits of aluminium, titanium, oxygen and silicon in larger amounts than could ever occur naturally, indicating that perhaps something unearthly was responsible for the cow's demise.

LEVITATING BULL

A retired Puerto Rican police officer was driving home in January 1997, when he saw a disc-shaped UFO levitating a bull with a beam of light. The bull vanished into the craft, which then flew away. When the man tried to follow the UFO, he was forced off the road by a truck. He claims that two Men In Black approached him, and told him to let them continue with their activities. This account is significant because it suggests a direct link between Men In Black, UFOs and cattle mutilation. A mutilated cow was found five hours later, some distance up the road.

SCORCH MARKS

In 1980, three people were injured after witnessing a UFO in Texas. After seeing the huge UFO, which they described as diamond-shaped and extremely bright, they all suffered from nausea, headaches, sunburn-like rashes and watery blisters. These symptoms lasted for several days, and one of the witnesses even lost hair from her head.

OZ INCIDENT

On May 28th 1965, an airliner flying from Brisbane to New Guinea was accompanied by a UFO for over ten minutes. Both the co-pilot and a stewardess were witness to the object. The pilot's photographs were confiscated before he could process them, and the aeroplane's flight-recorder was returned to Australia in secret.

UFO LANDING

In January 1989, circular traces of a UFO landing were found on the ground around a North American farm. The green chemical chlorophyll in the grass had been destroyed and the nutrients in the soil appeared to have been drained away. Fearing abduction, the family allowed UFO researchers to set up alarms around the house. These were set off a few nights later, waking the family who saw a ten metre (approximately 32 foot) UFO attempting to land nearby. This story was corroborated by an independent witness who saw the UFO from across the road.

GRAVE ROBBERS

The cemeteries around a church in Elk Garden, West Virginia, have been visited by many UFOs. In April 1968, Wayne Jones and his pregnant wife Brenda, were unable to sleep, and went out to check the cattle on their farm. As they drove out of town, Brenda spotted a light that appeared to have risen from under the ground. Their interest turned to fear when the small light joined other larger lights, and approached their car. They reported a 30 metre (approximately 100 foot) glowing ball of orange light hanging directly above the car. They drove away, but the light followed them, eventually giving up the chase, and hovering a short distance away. They roused their neighbours, the Jones family, who also witnessed the UFO over the farm. The craft moved rapidly from place to place for 30 minutes, occasionally pausing to spout flames from its perimeter. A month later, Wayne and Brenda's daughter Sheri was born, with an orange birthmark-circle on her body.

Amie Kalbaugh, another local resident, saw similar lights on many occasions over the following ten years — and they were always close to the churchyard. Her older sister, Vickie, saw a large craft hovering over the meadow between their house and the cemetery, and smaller lights rise from the ground towards it. It was suggested that the dead must have been abductees, and that aliens were coming back to remove implants. In which case it seems that most of the residents must have been abductees – every time a new grave was dug, the lights would appear within a couple of nights.

IMPLANT SURGERY

In 1995 a surgeon removed foreign bodies from two separate abductees, one female, one male. Abduction researcher Derrel Simms of Houston guided the surgeon Dr. Leir as they located and removed objects believed to be alien implants. The first patient had two objects removed, the second patient had one. Simms claims that even during his initial investigations, these people had no idea that they had been implanted. The patients felt no pain in the area where the objects were located and no scarring or tissue disturbance was evident – the implants were only discovered by x-ray. Working on the female patient first, Dr. Leir cut into her toe, and searched for the object. At one point he accidentally touched the implant with his scalpel, causing a powerful reaction in the woman, as though she had been hurt. This is extremely unusual under local anaesthetic, and suggests that the object was somehow linked to the woman's nervous system. The object removed from the woman's toe was a flat triangular shape about five millimetres (approximately quarter of an inch) long. Its surface was made up of a stiff, grey membrane which resisted being cut with a scalpel and was almost impossible to remove. A second object was seed-shaped and was very

similar to an implant removed from the back of the male patient's hand. Further studies showed that the implants were connected with living tissue via cloned cells and were attached to nerves. All the implants fluoresced brightly in ultraviolet light. Simms found that the implants were metallic, highly magnetic and composed of a dark, shiny material. The search is now on for more implants.

AREA 51

A secret base, known as Area 51 or Groome Lake, is located in the desert some distance from Las Vegas. The site was supposedly used to test the U-2 spyplane, but UFOs have often been seen in the area. Some people believe that dead aliens are kept here and that saucer technology is stored and tested here. It is possible that UFOs sighted in the area have been built by humans, based on knowledge gained from crashed saucers. Bob Lazar claims that he worked on location south of Area 51, back-engineering alien technology for use on Earth. Signs around the base warn that intruders may have to face 'the use of deadly force', indicating that the American government is keen to keep its secrets. In April 1997, a television broadcast showed footage of an alien being 'interviewed' at Area 51. It is claimed that the man who processed the video footage managed to smuggle a segment out. Although many people think that this is a hoax, they still believe that Area 51 is related to UFO activities. If the governments of the world are in touch with aliens, this may be where the secret meetings take place.

CRASH TEST DUMMIES

In June 1947 the US Air Force (USAF) tried to put an end to speculation about the Roswell flying saucer crash. They claimed that extensive research had shown that aliens were not involved in the incident. Once again they tried to convince the public that no saucer crashed, but that the 'wreckage' was simply debris from a top secret balloon, which was part of Project Mogul. This hasn't convinced many serious researchers, who point out that more than 500 witnesses have come forward to say that a flying disc *did* crash, and was recovered by the government. The USAF also claimed that 'alien bodies' seen near to the wreckage were just dummies dropped from balloons, as part of Air Force research. This story might be convincing, except that

such tests only began six years after the Roswell incident. This vast discrepancy makes it look as though the USAF are getting desperate in their attempts to cover up the truth.

CROP CIRCLES

CROP PICTURES

Although there are a few reports of ancient crop circles, most have formed since the late eighties. Over 400 swirled depressions have been found in farmers' crops, and many have been associated with UFOs. At first they were thought to be landing sites or 'saucer nests'. That theory was thrown out when the circles developed rings and corridors. During the nineties these pictograms began to represent spiral galaxies, scorpions, and chaos mathematics.

CORN CIRCLES?

Although crop circles are often referred to as 'corn circles' they have appeared in many crops. Circles have been found in peas, beans, rice, canola (oil-seed rape), oats, spinach, grass, linseed, maize, sunflowers, sugar beet, mustard, potatoes and rye. Most, however, form in wheat or barley. Maize, or 'corn' as it is known, is hardly ever patterned with circles.

WORLDWIDE CIRCLES

Crop circles have formed in France, Canada, India, America, Afghanistan, Germany, Sweden, Hungary, and many other countries. In Japan a circle even appeared in a rice paddy and a huge quantity of water was found to have been taken away, or evaporated. In other countries, snow circles have been sighted, and ice circles and rings have been found spinning in lakes, with no traces of human approach.

DOUG AND DAVE

In 1991 two men in their sixties from Hampshire, England, Doug Chorley and Dave Bower, claimed to have hoaxed many circles after having seen pictures of a real crop circle. Over the following years, many hoaxing teams were exposed, though none were ever caught in the act.

CIRCLEMAKERS

The teams of people who make crop circles, don't always regard themselves as hoaxers. They prefer to be called 'circlemakers', and claim that they make the crop circles as a form of sacred art. The circlemakers dress entirely in black as night-time camouflage. Many say they have seen bright, unexplained lights while circlemaking, or have seen balls of light moving around them as they flatten the crop. Julian Richardson, a circlemaker from Northampton, England, saw a UFO while rolling a formation near Cranford St. Andrew. He believes that the orange light which he spotted hovering above a nearby hill wasn't a flare as it appeared to be solid. When he spoke to other circlemakers in Wiltshire a few days later, he discovered that they had experienced similar things. Many believe that, even when hoaxed, crop circles attract UFOs.

HOAXING COMPETITION

A crop circle hoaxing competition was held in West Wycombe, England, during 1992. Each team was required to create the same pattern from a diagram drawn by the competition organisers. The circlemakers worked in the dark, silently, with equipment ranging from garden rollers and planks, through to bar stools and step ladders. The results ranged from unconvincing patterns, to realistic looking crop circles – proving that, even in the dead of night, it is possible to hoax elaborate formations.

DISTORTIONS

People who visit genuine crop circles often experience time distortions, sensory enhancements, feelings of peace — and many see UFOs. When actually inside circles visitors often find that cameras jam, video recorder batteries drain, compasses spin wildly, radios go dead and mobile phones malfunction. Ill effects such as headaches and nausea are common — and dogs have frequently been known to vomit when inside crop circles.

EXPLANATIONS

When crop circles first appeared, many explanations were put forward for them. So-called experts blamed causes as diverse as ball lightning, mating deer, wandering hedgehogs, helicopter downdraughts and electrified whirlwinds. Hoaxing was barely even considered, but as the circles became more and more complex it began to seem more likely. Researchers now believe that there are a mixture of hoaxed and genuine circles. In some cases, UFOs apparently copy hoaxed circles in nearby fields. The scale and complexity of recent formations, has led many people to conclude that hoaxing simply cannot account for the vast and intricate formations which form in a matter of minutes.

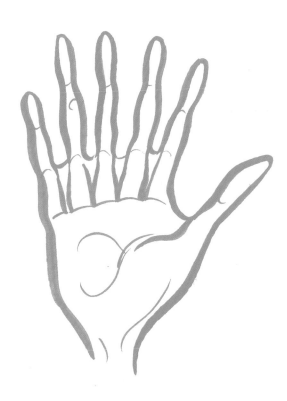

THE EYE

Crop circle researchers in England were present at an extraordinary event in Wiltshire's East Field in July 1994. They parked above the field, hoping to film a huge eye-shaped formation which had been swirled into the crop some days before. Before they reached the field, two military helicopters flew into view. The researchers felt that they were being filmed by one helicopter, while the other flew extremely low, almost hitting the hillside with its rotors. The researchers said there was a feeling of harassment, and felt they were being encouraged to leave the area. The helicopters changed their position, and headed over East Field itself. One flew so low that a researcher who was already in the formation threw himself to the ground. When the helicopter stopped and hovered over the field, a white, unidentified object was seen floating in front of it, just above the wheat.

LANDING SITE

Following the sighting of four burning balls of lights over North Head, Australia on February 19th 1997, reports came in of a crop circle formation. Spotted by a pilot on the outskirts of Werribee, Melbourne. The nine metre (approximately 30 foot) circle was swirled in a clockwise manner. Unlike most British crop circles, it had large indentations in the ground, reminiscent of landing marks. The six circular depressions were about ten centimetres (approximately four inches) deep, and were spread around the perimeter of the circle. The bottom of each hole was rounded, and the soil there was imprinted with a cross. Brown burn marks were also found on the crop, suggesting that something hot and heavy had landed in the field.

MAGIC BENDS

Genuine crop circles contain stems of wheat that are curved over in a gentle arc, rather than snapped, cut or kinked. These 'magic bends' appear to have been created by some high energy source – this is unhoaxable, but a similar effect *can* occur in hoaxed circles. When left for a few days, flattened wheat tries to climb towards the sun, and in doing so it bends perfectly. Many sceptics claim that all so-called 'magic bends' are nothing more than natural regrowth, although researchers claim that true magic bends are still found in some circles.

BENT BUT NOT BROKEN

Canola, or oil-seed rape, is an extremely brittle, sappy crop, and tests have shown that attempting to roll it over manually snaps the stalks. Hoaxers hate the crop, because pushing it down is as difficult as flattening a small forest. One of the best oil-seed circles formed in early 1997, near the ancient hill fort of Barbury Castle, England. It consisted of six half-moon crescents, and was nearly 60 metres (approximately 200 feet) long. There was no evidence of bruising on the stems. By contrast, a hoaxed formation which formed nearby a few days later, was full of snapped stems and bruises.

CIRCLE UFOs

Towards the end of summer 1996, video footage was secured which shows UFOs creating a crop circle. Two sets of glowing lights are seen to circle the field at dawn, and the circle forms in the wheat below them. The entire incident lasts just 19 seconds. The footage was first shown seven hours after the formation was found, and is extremely convincing. Even so, many researchers suspect it to be a hoax. The balls of light are not blurred from frame to frame, suggesting that they were added to the footage by computer. Other researchers have pointed out that camera-shake is seen throughout, which would make superimposing balls of light very difficult. The formation itself consisted of 18 circles, arranged in a snowflake pattern around a large central circle. While some observers claimed to find muddy footprints and evidence of hoaxing, others said that when first examined the circle was undamaged and perfectly clean, even though it had rained all night. Hoaxing on rainy nights is impossible, because mud always covers the stems. Unfortunately, the man who filmed the UFOs is unwilling to elaborate on his story, and has disappeared without a trace.

GIANT CIRCLES

Although many of the great formations are as much as 150 metres (approximately 500 feet) in diameter, it is unusual to find them any larger. Two exceptions are notable. In June 1996 a massive crop formation was found in a field of barley. Its main design was a long path, with small circles at either end and although quite ugly it measured an impressive 300 metres (approximately 1000 feet) long. Later that year, Etchilhampton in Wiltshire, England, was host to a formation that was more than one kilometre (approximately three-quarters of a mile) long. The one-and-a-half metre (approximately five foot) wide pathway was patterned with twelve large circles. People walking through the formation claimed to experience energy surges which left them feeling joyous.

THEMES

Each crop circle season has a distinctive theme. In 1993 most crop circles were 'pictograms' with several circles formed on a large line. During 1994 'scorpion' shapes were common, along with 'thought-bubbles' with lines of ever-decreasing circles. Multiple circle events were the main theme of 1995, with many formations containing over eighty circles, arranged in patterns representing solar systems, galaxies and asteroid belts. The circles of 1996 were mostly based on ancient glyphs and chaos physics. For 1997 the circles represented complex mathematics, fans, and magical symbols.

ALIEN COMMUNICATION

Two German researchers believed they had decoded the messages of crop circles in 1991, and hoaxed a pictogram using the same coded language in an attempt to contact the genuine circlemakers. Two pictograms that formed elsewhere, soon after, were thought to be the circlemakers' response. When decoded, these pictograms apparently pointed to a distant sun, with two small planets. It was also found that the Barbury Castle pictogram represented a star map, and even tiny details from the circle design, which seemed like imperfections, matched up with stars in this area of the sky. If aliens do make crop circles, it is just possible that they may be pointing out their home world.

COMET

During the winter of early 1994, a hoaxer in England spent hours planning crop circle designs for the coming season. One image created on his computer was of a crescent within a ring. His intention was to swirl the formation on the West of Waden Hill, but before he got the chance, the same design appeared across the road, in a similar field. The hoaxer has no idea how it got there, as nobody had seen his plans. It made him wonder if the 'real' circlemakers were trying to give him a message. Strangely, this same pattern of a crescent in a ring, appeared on the surface of Jupiter after the Schumacher-Levy comet crashed into it later that year.

JULIA SET

On July 8th 1996 a set of 151 circles measuring nearly 120 metres (approximately 400 feet), formed in a field opposite Stonehenge, England. It was an incredible sight at ground level, but even more astounding from the air. The main band of circles, which were spread over an  expanding arc, started small, grew to a great width and then diminished again. Each circle was adorned with curved arms of small circles. The pattern is believed to be a Julia Set Fractal, a visual representation of chaos mathematics. Fractal images have been found in crop circles before, most notably with the Mandelbrot set in 1991, but the Julia set even outshone that.

The Julia set was believed to have been formed during daylight hours. Apparently, a pilot passed over the field in the afternoon, when flying friends over Stonehenge; at that time the field was unpatterned. It is highly unlikely that people flying over the area could miss such a huge formation. When the pilot flew back, 45 minutes later the formation was present. This means it must have formed in broad daylight, next to a busy road.

DNA

Wiltshire's East Field is patterned with crop circles every year, and in 1996 it received a huge formation that looked like a strand of DNA. Measuring nearly 200 metres (approximately 650 feet), it was aligned between two ancient sights, where many UFOs have been seen in recent years. A local man, who was driving along the southern road below the field at 6.30am is adamant that the field did not contain the formation at that time. The formation was first seen at 6.45am, meaning that it must have formed within 15 minutes. Researchers also detected radio anomalies and bizarre electrostatic readings within the formation.

WINDMILL HILL

The most incredible crop circle to date formed on the morning of July 29th one-and-a-half kilometres (approximately one mile) north of the Avebury Stone Circle, England. From a distance it appeared to be three curved arms; closer aerial inspection showed that it was a spiralling arrangement of three merged Julia sets. The pattern was more than 300 metres (approximately 1000 feet) wide, containing 194 circles, from the massive to the tiny. It contained many hidden geometries, and every type of floor pattern and layering that has ever been recorded. Hoaxing seems unlikely in this case, because even if we assume that the hoaxers were in the field as soon as it went dark, and left at the moment of dawn they would have had to create a circle every two minutes. The smallest, most rushed and messy circles take at least a minute, and large ones, if made well, can take a good hour. Aligning them in this pattern, during darkness, would take many hours.

AIRSHIP ABDUCTION

The North American Algonquian Indians recount a legend which may be based on a UFO contact. The story concerns an 'flying basket' which descended from the sky, bearing twelve beautiful maidens. The Algonquian legend states that the 'basket' flew away when approached by a hunter, but accidentally left behind one of the maidens. The hunter married her and together they had a son; at this point she built her own flying craft and left him, powering its flight with a song. At a later date she was sent back by her people, to take specimens from earth. She then took the hunter back to her home planet, where he was treated to a banquet.

This story is interesting, because many aspects are similar to contemporary UFO abduction themes. Stories of alien-human interbreeding and hybrid offspring are quite common, and in many abduction accounts, people report being taken to the home-world of aliens, where they are fed well. The story also shows the 'aliens' taking samples, and using music. In several contemporary accounts of aliens, music has been used as a means of communication.

DROP ANCHOR

In the year 1211, a flying vehicle apparently dropped an anchor overboard, which snagged on a church roof in Cloera, Ireland. A similar mystery airship was said to have passed over Merkel, Texas in 1897, where its anchor became caught on a fence. In both cases, the anchors were cut free from the ropes, allowing the ships to fly away.

ANCIENT TECHNOLOGY

The mystery of alien intervention may not be a recent phenomenon. According to conventional theory, modern humans evolved about 100000 years ago, but

evidence of ancient technology has been found which completely contradicts this. One of the most stunning examples is a metal vase, found in Dorchester, Massachusetts, embedded in rock that is 600 million years old. A finding such as this suggests that humans, or other advanced beings, were present on earth millions of years earlier than conventional science believes.

Fossilised footprints were found in 3.6 million-year-old volcanic ash, in Tanzania, East Africa. A number of anthropologists have confirmed that these are definitely footprints of humanoids. If they aren't human footprints, then it's possible that aliens were on earth millions of years ago.

Hundreds of grooved metal balls have been found in South Africa, and are estimated to be 2.8 million years old. They are perfectly round, some with three

grooves around the equator. In France, a flat metallic tube was found in a 65 million-year-old chalk bed. Some researchers believe that such findings are evidence of an alien presence, rather than advanced human existence. It is possible that aliens have been visiting Earth for millions of years, guiding our evolution, and leaving occasional traces of their presence behind.

RETURN OF THE ANCIENTS

In 1948, just one year after the famous Roswell crash, an alien ship was rumoured to have crashed in Aztec, New Mexico. Apparently 14 to 16 aliens were removed from the undamaged saucer. The craft itself was over 30 metres (approximately 100 feet) in diameter and made of a strong material, patterned with Sanskrit-type glyphs. This material could not be heated or damaged with a drill. The aliens were just over one metre (approximately four feet) tall, had large, slanted eyes and webbed fingers. Instead of blood, their wounds seeped a clear liquid. It is rumoured that Dr. Robert Oppenheimer (the director of the Atomic Bomb project at Los Alamos) was called to the scene.

MARBLE MYSTERY

A block of marble was discovered at a depth of about 18 metres (approximately 60 feet) in a quarry near Philadelphia, USA. The surface was patterned with letters, which were raised from the surface, rather than carved into it – showing that something was capable of complex craftwork, millions of years before man was supposed to exist. Similar symbols were found imprinted into an English crop field in the early 1990s. Whatever was responsible for forming the symbols in rock may well continue to leave cryptic messages for us today.

BIBLE STORIES

The Bible contains many references to 'giants' which came from the sky – many people interpret these stories as evidence of ancient alien visitations. One of the most telling comes from the book of Samuel, it describes 'a battle in Gath, where was a man of great stature, that had on every hand six fingers, and on every foot six toes, four and twenty in number; and he also was born to the giant.' Many abductees have reported seeing six-fingered aliens. Interestingly, the word 'God' in Hebrew translates as 'those who came from the sky'. There's even an apparent description of a UFO abduction in the second book of Kings when, 'There appeared a chariot of fire, and horses of fire...and Elijah went up by a whirlwind into Heaven'. Ezekiel also describes a whirlwind craft, which shone with bright amber light, and carried four humanoids, which could have been aliens.

FLYING DRAGONS

Chinese records, thousands of years old, show that Emperor Hwang-ti was able to fly in a craft described as a 'celestial dragon', along with 70 of his subjects. A copper tripod was set up on a mountain-top, and was said to respond to the harmonies of the planets, enabling some form of powered flight.

LIGHT SHIPS

The Toradja people, who live in the mountains of the Indonesian island of Celebes, may once have been ruled by alien beings. They recount stories of a race of 'kings' who came to them by 'lightening-powered' ships from the sky. The people still build their houses to resemble the ancient ships, painting them with spirals of energy to represent the ships' power source. In modern times they have started building with corrugated iron, with the result that their houses look remarkably like a fleet of flying saucers!

FLYING CANOE

Natives of the Mangareva Islands tell stories of a 'flying canoe' which appeared to their ancestors. These craft were flown by mysterious 'priests' who were able to fly enormous distances in one day. Could it be that they were visited by aliens in cigar-shaped UFOs?

EGYPTIAN HELICOPTER

Excavations around Cairo have revealed a hieroglyphic message which has baffled Egyptologists, because it is unlike any other. Amongst the symbols there is a clear image of a helicopter, and a flying saucer with a tail. Another image looks distinctly like a submarine.

ANCIENT UFOs

Ancient Indian texts talk about flying machines known as 'Vimanas'. The most common craft had two decks, and were circular in shape with portholes and a dome. Vimanas were said to make a melodious sound, similar to the throbbing hum mentioned in present day UFO tales. And, just like modern UFOs, Vimanas came in a variety of shapes, from saucers to cylinders.

THE FACE ON MARS

In 1976 NASA's Viking Orbiter photographed the surface of Mars. In the Cydonia area of the planet they discovered a gigantic stone face, about one-and-a-half kilometres (approximately one mile) long, and enclosed in some kind of headdress or helmet. This headdress is striped, resembling those found on Egyptian mummy-cases and there seem to be fine structures in the mouth which could be teeth. 20 kilometres (approximately twelve miles) south-west of 'The Face', there is a grouping of artificial-looking objects known as 'The City'. 'The Fortress' is an enclosed space, with a regular pattern of indentations along its lower wall. Close to this is a five-sided pyramid, which is orientated almost exactly due south. Many other pyramids are located in the same vicinity.

The most astonishing aspect of these formations is that they are all situated in one locality, this indicates that they are not simply random shapes which happen to represent pyramids. The fact that so many are found together suggests that they may have been built by intelligent beings. In the distant past, on the morning of the Martian summer solstice, residents of 'The City' would perhaps have seen the earth rise out of the mouth of 'The Face', followed by the sun, just as the sign of Leo rose out of the earth-Sphinx's head, 10000 years ago. Could it be that one ancient civilisation is responsible for both structures? Some people believe that the complex was left by aliens as a message for us, and that more clues will be found on the actual surface of Mars.

LIFE ON MARS

In August 1996 scientists discovered evidence of life on Mars. The fossilised organism was found embedded in a meteorite which landed on earth. The fragment of Mars rock was probably knocked off the surface of the red planet by a larger meteorite or comet, before drifting in the solar system for thousands of years, and eventually landing on earth. The tiny organism is surrounded by organic compounds, which indicate that life was once present on Mars. Although life may have been bacterial millions of years ago, it is possible that humanoid life-forms could have eventually developed. If advanced life died out on Mars when the atmosphere was destroyed, as seems likely, it is possible that microbes, insects and small animals could still be living in remote areas of the planet, perhaps underground.

MARTIAN GLOBAL WARMING

Geographic evidence taken by the Viking Orbiter, suggests that 'The City' and 'The Face' were built on the edge of an ancient Martian sea. It is possible that the Martian eco-system was destroyed by global warming. At that point, the atmosphere was depleted, the ice-caps froze, and the Martians were forced to leave. It's possible that they colonised earth, which means our ancestors might not be apes, but aliens. Alternatively it's possible that the few aliens who managed to escape to earth, influenced our society, and passed on learning, before dying out.

MARS MOUNDS

Mounds have been observed in 'The City' on Mars – and on the plain surrounding it. They are about 30 metres (approximately 100 feet) high, and up to 210 metres (approximately 700 feet) wide. Strangely, they appear to have been constructed so that their shadows form sharp points. There are about 16 of them arranged with incredible geometric accuracy. A group of three forms a perfect isosceles triangle – a shape almost unknown in nature. The angles within this triangle (19.5°), are identical to angles measured in the architecture of another nearby pyramid. Vast computer simulations were used to study the probability of this pattern occurring by chance, and it was found to be less than one in 2000 million.

ENERGY ALIENS

The modern perception of flying saucers only came about once we had created our own flying metallic craft. Until then, UFOs were perceived as anything from gods to burning birds. Could it be that UFOs have always been the same, but our way of perceiving them has changed?

When people see UFOs, they assume that they are seeing craft flown by aliens, but it's possible that they are seeing rare sky-creatures. These sky-whales may exist in the upper atmosphere, only rarely travelling down towards earth, where they become visible because of lower magnetic frequencies. These bioforms might come down to earth to feed, topping-up on their reserves of energy. This would explain why they are often sighted close to power stations, and natural energy sources such as ley lines and stone circles. Many witnesses also say that UFOs are organic and flexible, and change shape. Although these movements would be impossible for a solid spacecraft, bioform creatures could easily stretch and flex in this way.

WET MOON

Jupiter's moon Europa could be home to thousands of underwater creatures. Recent observations from the Galileo space probe show chunks of ice, and crater-free patches of surface, suggesting a younger, thinner surface than was previously believed. It is possible that oceans exist below this icy surface. The icebergs are rotating, which could mean they are being swirled around by warm water – ideal conditions for life to evolve.

HOT LIFE

Scientists often say that life needs sunlight and oxygen to survive, and consequently we can only look for life on planets similar to earth. This idea was recently disproved, when worm-like creatures were found next to a volcano under the sea. The life-forms existed in water above boiling point, without sunlight or oxygen, feeding instead on sulphur. These conditions sound very similar to those on Europa, suggesting that life is quite possible there. It also shows that life can adapt to almost any conditions, not just those found on earth.

LIFE GOES ON

In early 1996, astronomers discovered two planets outside our solar system, one of which may have enough water to support familiar types of life. The planets are orbiting a star known as 70 Virginis, and are similar to a planet found orbiting 51 Pegasi. The planets are all within 40 light-years of earth – showing that life-bearing planets exist relatively close to us, and that life may in fact be extremely common throughout the universe...

Published by MQ Publications Limited
254-258 Goswell Road, London EC1V 7EB

Copyright © MQ Publications Limited 1998

Text © Christopher Kenworthy 1998
Illustrations © Roger O'Reilly 1998

ISBN: 1-897954-33-6

1 3 5 7 9 0 8 6 4 2

Designed by Senate

Printed and bound in Italy